RI

ALSO BY LOIS MATHIEU

Debut, Song for My Birth Mother (fiction, 2012)
The Next to Last Drink (fiction, 2012)
Women Under Siege (fiction, 2016)
Snow Raining on Glass (poetry, 2017)

RIBBONS OF LIGHT

Poems by

Lois Mathieu

Antrim House
Bloomfield, Connecticut

ISBN: 978-1-943826-94-0

First Edition, 2022

Printed & bound by Ingram Content Group

Book design by Rennie McQuilkin

Cover photograph by Mary Sullivan

Antrim House
860.519.1804
AntrimHouseBooks@gmail.com
www.AntrimHouseBooks.com
400 Seabury Dr., #5196, Bloomfield, CT 06002

In memory of my beloved parents
Raymond and Cecelia Roach Mathieu

Acknowledgments

Thanks to my friends from the Farmington Valley CT Poetry Society workshop, who helped me find the right words for several of the poems in this collection. My gratitude to Rennie McQuilkin, publisher of Antrim House, whose critical eye is always discerning. It is a joy to work with him.

TABLE OF CONTENTS

I've seen the stars fall from the sky
Holy Mother can't keep from crying.

Eric Clapton

RIBBONS OF LIGHT

Third Grade

The bell for recess rang
We scurried to the schoolyard
I asked Teddy if I could touch
The tight-knitted weave covering
The perfect dome of his head

He held his gaze firm as an icicle
Frozen against a winter sky
His face the color of my penny
His eyes bright as timber burning
Light in the dark of night

In class he was called from his seat
To stand before Miss Mean's
Routine of stoking his rage
That was the day he kicked a hole
In her waste bin and we sat in fear

Teddy raced home with his cousin Zerlene
With the speed of the great escape
It was hard to keep up with their pace
Running down the hands of the clock
Readying their course for another day

We sat in our seats frozen as ice
Lacking words to define the act
Our first experience with hate
Waited so long to construct the truth
Of what we learned in third grade

Carlethia

His name was long enough to parse
The syllables of life in third grade
A student enunciating words
He stood to name Rome's seven hills
And the stick-legged birds of Africa

He stood against the fence at recess
Gripping the metal rungs of cold
Eyeing the way the Earth moved
He stood taller than many a tree
With stories walking me halfway home

Before stepping into the gray-green sea
Of tar-paper buildings called *The Project*
Leaving me to trace the long migrations
Flamingos by the hundreds of thousands
Thirsting for Africa's water basins

The student became the prison Warden
His friendship gave me a compass to trace
The African journey closer to home
Four-hundred years thirsting for freedom
Beginning in third grade walking me home

Fourth Grade

Zerlene's brothers were James and Earl
Double trouble on a regular basis
They lived in the green tar-papered
Building between my home and where
My best friend lived and my bicycle was
Missing when I left her to go home
My mother drove me block by block

And saw the sun shine on the silver
And blue Samson leaning on its kickstand
I was brave enough to pedal it home
With my mother following close behind
Nothing more was ever said and time
Moved on with James and Earl and me
Remembering that day in fourth grade

Fifth Grade

The best way to walk home
Was to toss a coin
Into the wind and call
"Hey Bunky wait up!"

His smoky eyes brown and green
Angled bones impressed his acne face
Features sharp enough for camera-
Ready photos in a Hollywood magazine

Some believed he carried a knife
One boy in the neighborhood
Got close enough to tell the lie
More believable than the truth

Bunky left our school before the morning
Paper said he was taken to the jailhouse
His camera-ready face imprisoned
In the shadows of the color spectrum

Hand-Me-Down

Open the door to the cardboard
Doll house pieced together by design
See mother in her floral apron
Making dinner with high heels on

Arrange the rooms and stage the play
Sit the dollies on wooden chairs
The table is set with mother's praise
For building a future just like hers

Night Train to Vermont

Out of the deep valley of dream
Came the whistle of a train
Smoking through the meadowland

Where passion spent on youth
Grew promises by the hundreds
And we swirled them into buckets filled
With sap from winter's Sugar Maples

Dusk slipped in to steal the night
My dream turned suddenly to fear
I listened for your voice and heard

The ticket master call your name
As the train pulled out of the station
You kept your promise at the crack of dawn
When I felt your breath on the morning light

Loss

Pipes and fiddles fill the pews
To quiet the sound of emptiness

Beggar bowls lift to be filled
With the glory of his life

The sorrow in their hearts
Begging for one refrain

One more sound so clean and pure
To make life perfect again

Acorn Squash

From what I've read breaking-and-entering
Is a crime except for cutting into squash

The shiny husk of yellow-orange-green
Ripples over the core like a holiday spinning top

Stem curled skin smooth shell hard as nails
Halved so no one gets the bigger of the two

There is no crime in scooping out the unclaimed
Seed we let waste outside the vine

Inside we are but two halves sharing
One body hungering in November's cold

Charlestown

We went to see your Dad
And stayed all afternoon
He ordered pizza for our lunch
And brewed the coffee
That camouflaged the sound
Of hearts breaking

He invited us to view the treasures
Our sister had stored the week before
I wanted something she had worn
A pretty cardigan with buttons carved
A pair of golden earrings
A tiny owl from her collection

He handed me a pretty doll
I gave her as a bargaining tool
To keep her from reminding me
When we were seven and three
I talked her into giving up
Her favorite doll to me

And then we stood outside
Strained to say good-bye
He would go to meet a buddy
They would have a beer
And watch the tide release
Its promise to surge so high

He'd mind the waves recalling
What she'd said—I'm glad
the summer crowd has gone away!

We promised to keep in touch
Come anytime he said and showed us
Where to find the key

Hate

The way it creeps
Along the winding paths
Settles into cracks and hides
Inside the closed parentheses
Where habit-cloaked injustices
Embed in sheaf and leaf
And ink-stained pages
Of history's felled trees

The way it skulks
Inside the heaps and snares
Of old abandoned campfires
In wait for passersby
To kindle the stench of tinder
Their cigarettes still craving to be lit
Sparking flame with heat enough
To turn us into particles of dust

The Man Who Said

a loving tribute to Don

The day has come
And I admit
I want to be sober
And yet I cannot say
I want to stop drinking
Something wills me not
To budge the way of ice
Unable to thaw

I try to envision myself
With my eyes closed
Freely moving like a brook
Overflowing reshaping
Life breaking through
My long dark winter
On nothing more
Than a sliver of ice

When ice begins to melt
I venture out
On a conduit of light
Explore my hidden self
Travel on a ribbon of hope
Outside the safer boundaries
Far beyond the reach
Of my circular confinement

I approach the mystery but then
Turn back my face flushing in fear

I quiver in the trenches of my skin
Knowing that one day
I must turn myself in
I want to be sober but I cannot say
I want to stop drinking
I have the tiger by the tail

Winter has never been this frozen
Blue ice has imprisoned me
Far too long and I fear
My blood will never thaw
My mind takes comfort
In inactivity and the thought
Of venturing out begins
To close me in

But the late winter sun
Breaks through the ice
Its warmth stirs me to rise
I make my way to the surface
View myself from high ground
Seeing more than I want to see
Of my rusted-out circuitry
I need courage to thaw the pieces

Something unnamed carries me
Relief enables me to work
On troubles one at a time
Not overcome by the flood
Of all that I have done to myself
Cautiously I close the door
Stumble onto a glacial path
Frozen in ice I cannot speak

Cars creep into a graveyard
I watch the caretaker moving
Silently waiting for faucets to flow
Who knows what he carries
From one grave to another
No one is here to check his credentials
He watches the cars drive off
No flowers are left behind

Caught by the plummeting cold
My will grows ever weaker
A beacon of hope flashes its red
Neon light on the road ahead
Beckons me to follow the sign
A sign of life in the nighttime sky
Daring my weak and broken life
The way the infant sucks on hunger

I open the swinging door
Life and death greet me as before
The lights dimming to keep me
From the dark halls of my mind
I must find my way home
Before my circuitry closes down
I hear the call from Rumi's wandering soul
Who brought me here/And who will take me home

I wrestle myself to the ground
Dreaming of freedom burning
My life to the edge of the flame
In fields of desolation where
Incongruities shape the infinite
Bundling and swapping of synapses
I ask myself if life is better lived

Asleep or dead awake

My mind easily forms habits
Embeds them in its circuitous way
And hates giving them up
But many habits are not benign
I fear they will shadow me
What number am I on?
It's hard to forgive others
Harder yet to forgive myself

Depression
Overcomes me
A sudden wind shift
Assaults me from within
In an instant I am no longer
Connected to the world
I cannot move for fear
Of slipping into the dark abyss

All afternoon I hug the couch
In the aftermath of the cataclysm
Yesterday the promising sun
Cast diamonds on the sea
Today a demon has brought me
Here to view my empty grave
I have forgotten
The purpose of seasons

My psyche is disconnected
From the wholeness of being
Enclosed in the vacuum of depression
All day I lay in a dark cocoon
For fear of rankling my demons

I pray for a grace that will
Let me perform one simple
Act of the will

I keep one eye on my open grave
Slowly bring my cup to the sink
Wipe the table clean and a bowl of flowers
On clean white linen is all that I can muster
I try to remember my prayers but my catechism
Escapes me I forget the purpose of prayer
And I wonder if the sun will come up
In the morning

The cemetery pond is ice
Faucets are still frozen
People come and go in cars
And drop off pretty flowers
Cold bouquets shiver in the wind
The living should not linger here
But hasten from this frigid place
While the door is still open

Last night I arrived at a palace gate
Strolled down a path of sunlight
Leading to a massive door
A familiar garden bed
Carved the walk with stalks
Of parchment leaves with some
Bending over an oaken bench
And there I sat in the yellow light

Old habits and inclinations
Have lost their vigor
Useless now as dried paramecium

This burial is without ceremony
No flowers no cars
No people to bid farewell
The caretaker has gone home
But the faucets are flowing

Gravediggers come
Their shovels are set to turn
Me over into the raw umber
Old habits kick up as stones
It's not easy to bury the ego
Diggers seem not to notice
I keep one stone for myself
A gem set free in the thaw

They stop for a smoke
Move to the next grave
But I have come here
To lay my ego to rest
Ice is breaking up
The peaceful waters are spreading
To where I am free and alive
With new grass growing

Motoring

On the quiet river
I hear the sound
Of song then laughter
Imagine someone calling me
Perhaps I should reply

Voices stir my yearning
The way one sip of wine
Ignites the flame that steers
A willing soul
Into the headlight of desire

Too soon the music fades
The quiet river returns
To the sound of water slapping
Against the motoring hum
In time to paddle me home

New England

Summer's done
And Sparrows'
Tiny feet
Kick the stones
On sidewalks
In search of crumbs
While New England
Shutters itself
Against the cold

Winter will come
When all the leaves
Have fallen
When Sparrows light
As dry little sticks
Perch outside
My window ledge
For something more
Than Nature is willing

Thief

Gazing into the crystal pool
A distillate of the Irish Sea
Blue agate rims look back at me

Suddenly the thievery of cheeky
Water bugs interrupts the wonder
And skates off with my dreams

Rush Hour

I take the beeline route
And head for home
To find my life support
Sequestered in a box
Shivering in the cold

I open the lid and reach
Inside to unwrap the form
My mouth watering on its way
To the sweet delight
Of a monk-brown brownie

Spy

Beneath the sheet of a blue-white sky
Where the stone-gray water runs cold
The circles of a steel-cut body
Calculate the distance with a feather-
Vectored clock and precise mathematics
Targeting the bull's eye

Talons spread then backward glide
One sweep seizes the quivering gloss
A promise kept for the squawks inside
The nest wove tight as a Persian rug
Staying the course until the light of day
Turns black on the ribbon of night

ABOUT THE AUTHOR

Lois Mathieu, a Connecticut native, writes poetry and fiction. She earned a B.A. in Liberal Studies from Syracuse University and an M.A. in English from Trinity College. Thereafter, she worked in the corporate world as a manager of customer documentation and made friends across the globe during many working trips to Japan.

Lois Mathieu's poems have been issued by journals such as *Calyx, Connecticut River Review, Connecticut Poets at Work, Embers,* and *Portland Review.* They have also appeared in anthologies: the Texas Tech University Press anthology, *Blood to Remember, American Poets on the Holocaust;* and the Northwoods Press anthology, *Sweet as Hautboys, Green as Prairies.* Her poem "Counting Sheep by Night" won the Joseph E. Brodine Award presented by The Connecticut Poetry Society.

Lois has written poetry reviews for the journal *Gargoyle*; and she is the author of three novels: *Debut, Song for My Birth Mother; The Next to Last Drink* (named to *Kirkus Review's* Best of 2012 list); and *Women Under Siege;* as well as a book of poems, *Snow Raining on Glass.*

Lois is married to writer and theologian William L. Newell, Professor Emeritus at Eastern Connecticut State University. They live in West Hartford, CT, and have two children as well as four grandchildren.

This book is set in Garamond Premier Pro, which had its genesis in 1988 when type-designer Robert Slimbach visited the Plantin-Moretus Museum in Antwerp, Belgium, to study its collection of Claude Garamond's metal punches and typefaces. During the fifteen hundreds, Garamond – a Parisian punch-cutter – produced a refined array of book types that combined an unprecedented degree of balance and elegance, for centuries standing as the pinnacle of beauty and practicality in type-founding. Slimbach has created a new interpretation based on Garamond's designs and on compatible italics cut by Robert Granjon, Garamond's contemporary.

Copies of this book can be ordered
from all bookstores including Amazon.

•

For more information on the work of Lois Mathieu,
visit www.antrimhousebooks.com/authors.html.

CPSIA information can be obtained
at www.ICGtesting.com
Printed in the USA
LVHW092030110222
710699LV00027B/113

9 781943 826940